Article 5

The Child's Right to Appropriate Direction and Guidance

A Commentary on the United Nations Convention
on the Rights of the Child

Editors

André Alen, Johan Vande Lanotte, Eugeen Verhellen,
Fiona Ang, Eva Berghmans, Mieke Verheyde, and Bruce Abramson

Article 5

The Child's Right to Appropriate Direction and Guidance

By

Garton Kamchedzera

MARTINUS
NIJHOFF
PUBLISHERS

LEIDEN • BOSTON
2012

Cover illustration: Nadia, 1½ years old.

Library of Congress Cataloging-in-Publication Data

Sandifolo Kamchedzera, Garton.
   Article 5 : the child's right to appropriate direction and guidance / by Garton Kamchedzera.
      p. cm. — (Commentary on the United Nations Convention on the Rights of the Child)
   Includes bibliographical references.
   ISBN 978-90-04-14862-8 (pbk. : alk. paper) 1. Convention on the Rights of the Child (1989).
Article 5. 2. Children (International law) 3. Children's rights. 4. Guardian and ward. 5. Parent
and child (Law) I. Title. II. Title: Article five.

   K639.S26 2012
   344.03'27—dc23

                                                                                    2012001983

ISSN 1574-8626
ISBN 978 90 04 14862 8 (paperback)
ISBN 978 90 04 22800 9 (e-book)

This book is printed on acid-free paper.

Printed by Printforce, the Netherlands

CONTENTS

LIST OF ABBREVIATIONS

ACRWC	African Charter on the Rights and Welfare of the Child
AIDS	Acquired Immunodeficiency Syndrome
CEDAW	Convention on the Elimination of All Forms of Discrimination against Women
CRC	Convention on the Rights of the Child
CRC Committee	Committee on the Rights of the Child
DAP	Developmentally Appropriate Practice
HIV	Human Immunodeficiency Virus
ECtHR	European Court of Human Rights
CCPR	International Covenant on Civil and Political Rights
CESCR	International Covenant on Economic, Social, and Cultural Rights

AUTHOR BIOGRAPHY

Garton Kamchedzera is a former Dean at the Faculty of Law, University of Malawi, where he is associate professor of law. He is a legal and development consultant, with wide and deep experience in child rights, human rights-based approach to development, inter-generational equity, law reform, customary law, peace, the rule of law, justice indicators, gender, governance, law and impoverishment, civil society and development, programme and project design and evaluation, and development-related research.

In addition to university teaching and research, his work has been with United Nations Country Teams, United Nations agencies, many African, Asian and European governments, the European Union, many international and national development agencies, and communities and children. From 1999 to 2001, he was Head of Social Policy, Advocacy, and Communication for UNICEF-Malawi during which time he led several key activities for UNICEF-Malawi and within the United Nations Development Assistance Framework. He was a key member of the team that formulated, piloted, and developed a human rights-based approach to development programming for UNICEF and its partners in East and Southern Africa. He has served on many boards, committees, and commissions in and outside Malawi.

He has researched and published on child and human rights, dignified life, and law and development. His research has encompassed many countries, including Botswana, Sierra Leone, Tanzania, Zimbabwe, Malawi, Papua New Guinea, Ethiopia, Finland, Nicaragua, Iraq, Uganda, Ghana, and Liberia. He has held and still holds several editorial positions.

His PhD from the University of Cambridge, England, completed in 1996, was on the holding, management, and control of property resources to realize child rights in poor social units. He also holds an LL.M from the University of Warwick, the United Kingdom, and an LL.B (Hons) from the University of Malawi.

TEXT OF ARTICLE 5

ARTICLE 5

States Parties shall respect the responsibilities, rights and duties of parents or, where applicable, the members of the extended family or community as provided for by local custom, legal guardians or other persons legally responsible for the child, to provide, in a manner consistent with the evolving capacities of the child, appropriate direction and guidance in the exercise by the child of the rights recognized in the present Convention.

ARTICLE 5

Les Etats parties respectent la responsabilité, le droit et le devoir qu'ont les parents ou, le cas échéant, les membres de la famille élargie ou de la communauté, comme prévu par la coutume locale, les tuteurs ou autres personnes légalement responsables de l'enfant, de donner à celui-ci, d'une manière qui corresponde au développement de ses capacités, l'orientation et les conseils appropriés à l'exercice des droits que lui reconnaît la présente Convention.

CHAPTER ONE

INTRODUCTION

1. This commentary both joins and transcends previous ones[1] on Article 5 of the Convention on the Rights of the Child (CRC).[2] It joins previous commentaries to elucidate the meaning of the Article, which has no State reservation against it.[3] It however transcends those commentaries in three ways. First, this commentary identifies and resolves misleading points from previous commentaries. Second, the commentary adopts a child rights-based approach in its analysis of the Article, other standards, previous works, and practices. Third, the commentary uses the concept of progressive dignified life for the child as an analytical and organizing idea.

2. Progressive dignified life, as an aspect of well-being, is one obvious reason for child rights and the CRC. As a notion, dignified life entails the existence of conditions that are conducive to the enjoyment of human dignity, which is inherent in every person. As an aspect of well-being, dignified life connotes "the enjoyment of human rights, compliance with and advancement of human rights principles, and the performance of duties correlative to specific human rights."[4]

3. The notion of dignified life is hence strongly implied in the CRC, which contains the human rights of children, child rights principles, and the performance of state and other obligations. In this sense, the CRC is not just about the well-being of children, but their dignified lives. This is a useful way to understand the concept of well-being, which is present in the CRC,

---

[1] *E.g.*, S. Detrick, *A Commentary on the United Nations Convention on the Rights of the Child* (The Hague, Martinus Nijhoff Publishers, 1999); P. Alston, 'The Legal Framework of the Convention on the Rights of the Child', *United Nations Bulletin of Human Rights* 91/2, 1992, pp. 1–15; R. Hodgkin and P. Newell, *Implementation Handbook for the Convention on the Rights of the Child* (New York, UNICEF, 2002), pp. 85–94.

[2] United Nations, Convention on the Rights of the Child, adopted on 20 November 1989, entered into force on 2 September 1990, http://www.ohchr.org/english/law/crc.htm.

[3] United Nations, Declarations and Reservations to the Convention on the Rights of the Child, http://www.ohchr.org/english/countries/ratification/11.htm#reservations.

[4] Garton Kamchedzera and Chikosa Ulendo Banda, 'Dignified Rural Living, the Right to Development, and Multiparty Politics in Malawi', (2009) 25 *South African Journal of Human Rights* 73, at 73.

most expressly in its Preamble and Articles 3(2), 9(3), 17, and 40(4). In Article 3, the CRC links well-being with the duties and responsibilities of parents and other carers, a theme expressly accentuated in Articles 5, 18, and 27.

4. Well-being itself is determined by three crucial aspects. The first is *what* every human being must enjoy, expressed as rights in the CRC. The second is *how* every human being should be treated with regard to approaches, attitudes, and modes of decision and action-taking. This question of *'how'* is in human rights discourse addressed by human rights principles such as non-discrimination. The third determinant of well-being is what people *should do*, or duties, regarding their and others' well-being. Article 4 requires progressive realisation of the rights in the CRC, regarding economic, social, and cultural rights. This implies that the state of child well-being has to be progressive.

5. Dominant theories of well-being do not adequately capture the essence of human rights, human rights principles, and duties correlative to human rights as critical determinants for children's dignified life. Child rights though provide a critical test case to the credibility of any such theories.[5] Sen[6] and *The Human Development Report*[7] focus on the exercise of choice and freedom, difficult to apply to very young children. Griffin's happiness theory of 'prudential perfectionism'[8] is not holistic enough to encompass all people, especially children. It also fails to take into account the importance of human rights principles and performance of duties. More holistic methods, such as the University of Helsinki's method of underlining 'having, loving, and being',[9] the Canadian emphasis on 'being', 'belonging', and 'becoming',[10] and *The Economist Magazine*'s use of subjective life satisfaction surveys and objectively obtained indicators to produce well-being tables for countries[11] are all useful. However, all these attempts appear haphazard in the

---

[5] N. McCormick, *Legal Right and Social Democracy* (Oxford, Oxford University Press, 1982), p. 154.

[6] A. Sen, *Development as Freedom* (Oxford, Oxford University Press, 1999).

[7] UNDP, *Human Development Report 2000* (Oxford/New York, Oxford University Press, 2000).

[8] J. Griffin, *Well-being, Its Meaning, Measurement and Moral Importance* (Oxford, Oxford University Press, 1988).

[9] E. Allardt, 'Having, Loving and Being: An Alternative to the Swedish Model of Research', in: M.C. Nussbaum and A. Sen (eds.), *The Quality of Life* (Oxford, Oxford University Press, 1993), pp. 88–94.

[10] 7th Generation Initiative, *Measuring Well-Being*, http://www.flora.org/sustain/well-being.shtml.

[11] The Economist, *The Economist Intelligence Unit's quality-of-life index*, http://www.economist.com/media/pdf/QUALITY_OF_LIFE.pdf.

selection of indicators, especially regarding the dignity of children. Pogge's use of the concept of 'human flourishing'[12] misses the importance of human rights principles, let alone child rights principles, in the determination of attitudes, approaches, processes, and practices. It further ignores the interconnectedness of duties correlative to human rights at all societal levels.

6. The concept of progressive dignified life for the child largely determines this commentary's methodology. In the main, the approach is child rights-based, examining the content of the CRC's Article 5, correlative duties, and implications of the need to comply with child rights principles. Focusing on dignified life, the commentary is necessarily contextual, exploring implications in an increasingly globalizing world and changing communities.

7. The commentary uses both primary and secondary sources. These include the CRC and other related international instruments. The commentary further uses the work of the Committee on the Rights of the Child[13] (CRC Committee) as manifested through general comments, concluding observations, and records of Days of General Discussion. The commentary furthermore makes references to national-level sources such as constitutions and decided cases.

8. This introduction of the commentary is followed by an examination of the text of the Article in the context of related international and regional human rights standards. The bulk of the commentary is about the scope of the Article. Each of its tenets is interpreted and implications indicated. The last part is the conclusion, which underlines that Article 5 is a potentially useful revolutionary normative resource for the progressive dignified life of children.

---

[12] T. Pogge, *World Poverty and Human Rights* (Cambridge, Polity Press, 2002), chapter 1.
[13] CRC Committee, http://www.ohchr.org/english/bodies/crc/.

CHAPTER TWO

COMPARISON WITH RELATED INTERNATIONAL HUMAN RIGHTS PROVISIONS

9. Article 5 of the CRC is both similar to and distinctive from other related international and regional standards. Such similarity and distinctiveness mirror the background debates during its drafting process.[14] The initial draft of the Article was modified after observations that its thrust on the respect that should be accorded to parents was somewhat redundant in the light of earlier international norms and some norms in the then draft Convention.[15] Subsequent changes to the draft provision shifted the focus to the evolving capacities of the child and parental rights, duties and responsibilities.[16]

2.1 Article 5 and Directly Related CRC Provisions

10. As a provision similar to others in the CRC, it is essential to underline that Article 5 has to be read in its context, as part of the CRC. The CRC contains two categories of standards that more directly relate to Article 5 than others. The first category includes those standards that are often grouped together with Article 5. Since the CRC Committee indicated that State Party reports should report on Articles 5, 18(1-2), 9-11, 19-21, 25, 27(4), and 39 of the CRC under the heading of 'Family Environment and Alternative Care',[17] Article 5 has been frequently associated with those Articles.[18] However the common tenet in all these Articles is not so much their reference to 'family' or 'parents' or 'parent.' Indeed two of the Articles, 11 and 25, do not refer to these terms. These two Articles respectively deal with the need to combat illicit transfer of children and periodic review when a child is placed in an

---

[14] *Travaux Préparatoires* (UN Docs. E/CN.4/1987/25, 1989, paras. 24–26; E/CN.4/1988/28, 1988, paras. 7–9; UN Doc. A/CN.4/1989/48, 1989, paras. 31–32); reproduced in S. Detrick (ed.), *The United Nations Convention on the Rights of the Child: A Guide to the 'Travaux Préparatoires'* (London, Martinus Nijhoff Publishers, 1992), pp. 157–162.

[15] *Ibid.*

[16] *Travaux Préparatoires* (UN Doc. A/CN.4/1989/48, 1989), paras. 31–32, o.c.

[17] CRC Committee, *General Guidelines Regarding the Form and Content of Initial Reports to Be Submitted by States Parties Under Article 44, paragraph 1(a), of the Convention* (UN Doc. CRC/C/5, 1991).

[18] *E.g.*, State Party reports at http://www.unhchr.ch/tbs/doc.nsf.

alternative care environment. The shared thrust in the Articles is the need to nurture the child for her or his survival, development, participation, and protection.

11. The second category of CRC Articles more directly related to Article 5 is of those that uniquely refer to the notions of direction and guidance and the child's evolving capacities. Two Articles stand out in this regard. Article 14(2) of the CRC places a duty on States to 'respect the rights and duties of parents and, when applicable, legal guardians, to provide direction to the child in the exercise of [the freedoms of thought, conscience, and religion] in a manner consistent with the evolving capacities of the child.' On its part, Article 12(1) of the CRC's similarity to Article 5 is about the need to give due weight to the views of the child 'in accordance with the age and maturity of the child.' Both age and maturity are instructive indicators of the child's evolving capacities.

12. The non-repetition of similar terms in other provisions in the CRC does not entail that parental guidance and the child's evolving capacities should be restricted to Articles 12 and 14 of the CRC. The reason for this argument is that Article 5 relates to 'the exercise by the child of the rights recognized' in the CRC. In this regard, the apparent explicit reference in Articles 12 and 14 is only for emphasis or to dispel doubt.

2.2   Article 5 and Other International Standards

13. The uniqueness of Article 5 of the CRC is prominent when compared with other non-CRC international standards on child rights or child well-being. Its linking of the child's evolving capacities with appropriate direction and guidance is absent in all other comparable international human rights standards passed before and after 1989, when the CRC was adopted. In this regard, the CRC's Article 5 remains unique in international law.

14. Prior to 1989, the international law on child well-being was more inclined towards families than to children. Indeed during the drafting process, the early USA and Australia-led attempt was to make the Article protect families and parental autonomy.[19] The early approach was gradually changed in a quest for innovation and value-added. The innovation was found in the new focus on the need to recognize the child's evolving capacities as parents exercise direction and guidance for the child.

---

[19]   *Travaux Préparatoires* (UN Doc. E/CN.4/1987/25, 1987), paras. 24–26, o.c.

Universal Instruments

15. None of the other very few global human norms that resemble the CRC's Article 5 reflects the tenet of the child's evolving capacities. Article 23 of the International Covenant on Civil and Political Rights (CCPR) and Article 10 of the International Covenant on Economic, Social, and Cultural Rights (CESCR) stress the protection of the family. Article 18 of the CCPR stresses respect for 'the liberty' of parents and guardians in determining the religious and moral education of their children, without mention of the child's evolving capacities.[20] The CESCR[21] reflects a similar position. The Convention on the Elimination of All Forms of Discrimination against Women (CEDAW)[22] stresses shared responsibilities between fathers and mothers in the upbringing of children. The Universal Declaration of Human Rights'[23] pronouncement of the family as the natural and fundamental group unit of society is repeated in the other two instruments of the International Bill of Human Rights, but without reference to the child's evolving capacities. The CRC, on its part, recognizes that 'the family [is] the fundamental group of society and the natural environment for the growth and well-being of ... children.'[24] However, unlike the CRC, the image of the child as a rights holder who exercises rights is merely implied under the International Bill of Human Rights.

Regional General Instruments

16. The CRC's Article 5 is a break from the largely welfarist approaches expressed in regional general human rights instruments. Those standards underline the protection and dependency of the child and the need to protect and provide for her or him on the part of parents, society and the State. The strong emphasis in Article 5 on the subjectivity and participation of the child is certainly absent in the general regional standards. In Africa, the bias has been on the family as compared to the child. The African Charter on

---

[20] United Nations, International Covenant on Civil and Political Rights, adopted on 16 December 1966, entered into force on 23 March 1976, http://www.ohchr.org/english/law/ccpr.htm.

[21] United Nations, International Covenant on Economic, Social and Cultural Rights, adopted on 16 December 1966, entered into force on 3 January 1976, http://www.ohchr.org/english/law/cescr.htm.

[22] United Nations, Convention on the Elimination of All Forms of Discrimination against Women, adopted on 18 December 1979, entered into force on 3 September 1981, http://www.ohchr.org/english/law/cedaw.htm.

[23] United Nations, Universal Declaration on Human Rights, adopted on 10 December 1948, http://www.unhchr.ch/udhr/lang/eng.htm.

[24] Preamble of the CRC.

Human and People's Rights[25] repeats the notion in the CPPR that the family is the natural unit and basis of society that must be protected. The Charter adds that the family is 'the custodian of morals and traditional values.'[26] In this regard, every person has duties towards the family and must 'preserve the harmonious development of the family and work for the cohesion and respect' of the family and parents.[27] A Protocol to the Charter, on women's rights, has underlined that both parents have the primary responsibility to bring up children, with the state and the private sector having a 'secondary responsibility.'[28]

17. The general human rights standards in the Americas stress the importance of respecting parents and families. Hence whilst it is the duty of 'every person to aid, support, educate and protect his [or her] minor children', children have a duty 'to honour their parents always and to aid, support and protect them when they need it.'[29] Parents have a right 'to provide for the religious and moral education of their children or wards. . . . in accordance with their own convictions.'[30] The Additional Protocol to the American Convention on Human Rights in the Area of Economic, Social and Cultural Rights[31] underlines the need to protect the child on the part of the 'family, society and the State.'

18. The well-resourced human rights legal system of Europe is notable for its weakness on child rights[32] and strength on the protection of family life,

---

[25] African Union, African Charter on Human and Peoples' Rights, adopted on 27 June 1981, entered into force on 21 October 1986, http://www.africa-union.org/root/au/Documents/Treaties/Text/Banjul%20Charter.pdf.

[26] Article 18 of the African Charter.

[27] Article 29 of the African Charter.

[28] African Union, Protocol to the African Charter on Human and Peoples' Rights on the Rights of Women in Africa, adopted on 11 July 2003, entered into force on 25 November 2005, http://www.africa-union.org/root/AU/Documents/Treaties/Text/Protocol%20on%20the%20Rights%20of%20Women.pdf, Article 13(l).

[29] Organization of American States, American Declaration of the Rights and Duties of Man, adopted on 2 May 1948, http://www.oas.org/documents/eng/documents.asp.

[30] Organization of American States, American Convention on Human Rights, adopted on 22 November 1969, entered into force on 18 July 1978, http://www.oas.org/documents/eng/documents.asp.

[31] Organization of American States, Additional Protocol to the American Convention on Human Rights in the Area of Economic, Social and Cultural Rights ('Protocol of San Salvador'), adopted on 17 November 1988, entered into force on 16 November 1999, http://www.oas.org/juridico/english/Treaties/a-52.html, Article 16.

[32] P. Alston and J. Tobin, Laying the Foundations for Children's Rights (Florence, UNICEF, 2005), pp. 16–21.

with equal responsibilities expected from parents.[33] Much jurisprudence has developed, but mostly about the rights of parents and other adults to family life. Fortin has noted that there is little case law from Europe that acknowl edges that children have human rights.[34] It is stated that the parent's freedom or right to bring up children in her or his own way is an important tenet in liberal democracy.[35] Accordingly, much European scholarship on parental authority has often been within the context of the right to a family life.[36] Unlike in the Americas, where human rights tribunals have an acknowledged record of using the CRC to interpret regional standards,[37] the European Court of Human Rights has been inward-looking. It has placed much importance on parental and similar rights, particularly the right to family life.[38] However, there is a Committee of Ministers Recommendation, agreed in 1984, that attempts to set standards on the resolution of issues pertaining to parental responsibilities.[39]

Regional Specific Instruments

19. Even regional standards that are specific on child rights fail to match the challenges implied in Article 5 of the CRC. It is true that the African Charter on the Rights and Welfare of the Child (ACRWC)[40] in its Article 20 usefully lists general duties expected from parents and other key carers. However, the ACRWC does not have a direct equivalent of the CRC's Article 5. The closest in wording to the CRC's Article 5 is a corresponding provision of

---

[33] G. Van Bueren, 'The International Protection of Family Members' Rights as the 21st Century Approaches', *Human Rights Quarterly* 17, No. 4, 1995, p. 735.

[34] J. Fortin, 'Accommodating Children's Rights in a Post Human Rights Act Era', *Modern Law Review* 69, No. 3, 2006, pp. 299–326.

[35] B. Hale, 'Understanding Children's Rights: Theory and Practice', *Family Court Review* 44, No. 3, 2006, pp. 350–360.

[36] European Court of Human Rights (ECtHR), *Kroon and Others v. the Netherlands*, 27 October 1994, *Publications of the Court*, Series A, 297-C.

[37] P. Alston and J. Tobin, *o.c.*, pp. 14–16.

[38] *E.g.*, European Court of Human Rights, *Rieme v. Sweden*, 22 April 1992, *Publications of the Court*, Series A, 226-B; *Keegan v. Ireland*, 26 May 1994, *Publications of the Court*, Series A, 290; *X, Y and Z v. the United Kingdom*, 22 April 1997, *Reports*, 1997-II; *Margareta and Roger Andersson v. Sweden*, 25 February 1992, *Publications of the Court*, Series A, 226-A.

[39] Council of Europe, Committee of Ministers, Recommendation No. R(84)4 of the Committee of Ministers to Member States on Parental Responsibilities, adopted on 28 February 1984. http://www.coe.int/t/e/legal_affairs/legal_co-operation/family_law_and_children's_rights/Documents/Rec_84_4.pdf

[40] African Union, African Charter on the Rights and Welfare of the Child, adopted on 11 July 1990, entered into force on 29 November 1999, http://www.africa-union.org/root/au/Documents/Treaties/Text/A.%20C.%20ON%20THE%20RIGHT%20AND%20WELF%20OF%20CHILD.pdf.

Article 14 of the CRC. Article 14 requires State Parties to respect the rights and duties of 'parents, and where applicable, legal guardians to provide direction and guidance' regarding the freedoms of conscience, thought, and religion.[41] Further, unlike in the CRC's Article 5, there is no reference to the extended family or community. This is an anomalous position for a continent still characterized by extended family ties, albeit attenuated by the cash economy and increased mobility. Furthermore, with regard to the participation of the child, the equivalent provision to Article 5 is the requirement that the child should 'work for the cohesion of the family, to respect his parents, superiors and elders, at all times and assist in case of need.'[42]

20. It could be argued, however, that the Charter's adoption of the principle that the best interests of the child should be 'the'[43] primary consideration entails that the required protection of the family and parents is a strategy to ensure progressive dignified life for the child. This construction of the Charter would entail that the 'duties' for the child enumerated in Article 31, are merely areas requiring parental guidance. This would mean that the duty to account, for the enumerated duties, should be with the parents until the child becomes an adult. It would also mean that the ACRWC's Article 10 entails prevalence of the child's best interests. That Article stipulates that parents have rights to exercise reasonable supervision over the conduct of their children with regard to the right to privacy.[44] Such interpretation of the ACRWC, however, is impossible without the use of the CRC's Article 5 as an aid in construction.

21. Apart from the ACRWC, the other set of child rights-specific regional standards is the European Convention on the Exercise of Children's Rights.[45] Considering that Article 5 of the CRC is very much about appropriate direction and guidance regarding the 'exercise' of child rights, the title of this post-1989 European Convention is promising. However, the content of the European Convention itself has no direct bearing on the CRC's Article 5, except with regard to 'proceedings affecting [children] before a judicial body.'[46] This European Convention thus grants the child the rights to be

---

[41] Article 9(2–3) of the ACRWC.
[42] Article 31(1) of the ACRWC.
[43] Article 4(1) of the ACRWC.
[44] Article 10 of the ACRWC.
[45] Council of Europe, European Convention on the Exercise of Children's Rights, adopted on 25 January 1996, entered into force on 1 July 2000, http://conventions.coe.int/Treaty/en/Treaties/Html/160.htm.
[46] Article 1(2) of the European Convention.

informed and express views and the right to appoint special representatives in proceedings.[47] Thus this European Convention is parochial, at best more of an amplification of the CRC's Article 14 than it is about Article 5 and others in the CRC.

---

[47] Articles 4 and 5 of the European Convention.

CHAPTER THREE

SCOPE OF ARTICLE 5

22. The drafting history of Article 5 of the CRC shows that the framers were agreed on at least one major revolutionary point. They wanted to use the Article to introduce an innovation in international and national laws, systems, and processes for a child rights-focused approach to appropriate direction and guidance.[48] The recognition of the importance of parents and key carers to guide the child was not new in 1989. With the benefit of hindsight, however, the innovation was to emanate from three bases. The first was the need to take into account the evolving capacities of the child when providing appropriate direction and guidance in the child's enjoyment of human rights. The second was the centrality of a child rights approach in that appropriate direction and guidance would not merely be welfarist, but in the recognition that the child is a subject or holder of human rights that she or he should exercise. The third was a necessary introduction of the need to delineate the scope of parental authority and discretion, as the child enjoys her or his rights.

3.1 The Child's Right to Receive Appropriate Direction and Guidance

23. Being in the CRC, Article 5 is primarily about child rights. In human rights discourse, the child is a rights holder. Certain previous commentaries and a usual heading of the Article's marginal notes though have characterized Article 5 as being about 'parental guidance.'[49] The correct view is that parental guidance is one form of 'appropriate direction and guidance.' The observation that parents, guardians and other carers have a duty to guide and direct the child's enjoyment of her or his rights[50] has to be supplemented with the point that every duty has a correlative right, as Hohfeldian's[51] analysis illustrates. In this regard, the correlative right is

---

[48] *Travaux Préparatoires* (UN Doc. E/CN.4/1987/25, 1987), especially para 104, *o.c.*
[49] *E.g.*, R. Hodgkin and P. Newell, *o.c.*, p. 85; S. Detrick, *o.c.*, p. 115.
[50] S. Detrick, *o.c.*; P. Alston, *l.c.*, pp. 1–15; R. Hodgkin and P. Newell, *o.c.*, pp. 85–94.
[51] W.N. Hohfeld, 'Some Fundamental Legal Conceptions as Applied to Judicial Reason', *Yale Law Journal* 16, No. 23, 1913.

for the child, to receive appropriate direction and guidance from parents, guardians and other key carers. The Committee on the Rights of the Child in a General Comment on Early Childhood has well-captured the point that all children are entitled to, 'in accordance with their evolving capacities, the progressive exercise of their rights.' The Committee clarified:

> The Convention requires that children, including the very youngest children, be respected as persons in their own right. Young children should be recognized as active members of families, communities and societies, with their own concerns, interests and points of view. For the exercise of their rights, young children have particular requirements for physical nurturance, emotional care and sensitive guidance, as well as for time and space for social play, exploration and learning.[52]

24. In other words, the parent or key carer is, according to Article 5, a key participator in and not the determiner of the child's life. As a holder and exerciser of the right, the child is an active actor in both direction and guidance. The parent or carer is expected by the Article to be sensitive to the child's evolving capacities, preferences, and environment. Such environments include households, families, and cultural contexts. As Woodhead has underlined, there is need for

> recognition of young children as social actors, whose development is facilitated through social relationships, and active participation under the guidance of sensitive and listening adults.[53]

25. Unfortunately, hitherto, undue focus has been on the child's contexts and parental duties, to the neglect of the child's right in Article 5 of the CRC. In some of the analyses, the deliberate break from conventional liberal international approaches has not been observed. Commentators have instead adopted an adult-centred liberal relativism approach to the notions of family and parenthood, in some cases ignoring the content of the child's right in Article 5.[54] The family has been noted as understood to be in different forms in the world and consisting of different types. Nuclear, marriage-based, grandparent-headed, single parent, child-headed, heterosexual, same sex, and divorced are among many adjectives that have been

---

[52] CRC Committee, *General Comment No. 7, Implementing Child Rights in Early Childhood* (UN Doc. CRC/C/GC/7/Rev.1, 2006), para. 5.

[53] M. Woodhead, 'Early Childhood Development: a Question of Rights', *International Journal of Early Childhood* 37, No. 3, 2005, pp. 79–98, at 15.

[54] E.B. Silva and C. Smart (eds.), *The New Family* (London, Sage Publications, 1999); N. Bala and R.J. Bromwich, 'Context and Inclusivity in Canada's Evolving Definition of the Family', *International Journal of Law, Policy and the Family* 16, 2002, pp. 145–180.

used to describe the forms of families.[55] International law's choice not to define 'family' has been noted and Article 5 of the CRC observed as providing a flexible conception of 'family.'[56] In such a logic, traditional families, 'partnerships', 'visiting relationships', and other new forms through which people may nurture their children have been noted. Thus an adult-centred liberal relativism approach to the notion of family has been advocated to embrace a wide scope of families including non-conjugal 'close personal adult relationships.'[57] Others have underlined that the family is increasingly characterized by its 'legal and social fragmentation.'[58]

26. Similarly, a child-centred liberal approach to the understanding of parenthood has been advocated and the decline of marriage-based parenthood noted, especially with regard to countries of the North.[59] Absent, visiting, foster, adoptive, and step are some of the adjectives increasingly being used to qualify parenthood. Giddens has observed that many of the changes and debates, about sexuality and the future of families and family life, are manifestations of an increasingly globalizing world.[60] Giddens has long argued that globalisation is not just an economic phenomenon or just about big systems such as international markets. Instead, globalisation is a political, technological, cultural, economic phenomenon that also affects and influences intimate and personal aspects of life.[61] In this sense, the transformation of the traditional family system, including new forms of parenthood, is according to Giddens, part of a "truly global revolution in everyday life" whose "consequences are being felt around the world in spheres from work to politics."[62]

---

[55] *E.g.*, N. Bala and R. Bromwich, *l.c.*

[56] R. Hodgkin and P. Newell, *o.c.*, pp. 85–94.

[57] *E.g.*, House of Lords, *Fitzpatrick* v *Sterling Housing Association*, 28 October 1999, http://www.publications.parliament.uk/pa/ld199899/ldjudgmt/jd991028/fitz01.htm; D.A. Skinner and J.K. Kohler, 'Parental Rights in Diverse Family Contexts: Current Legal Developments', *Family Relations*, 51, 2002, pp. 293–300; E.B. Silva and C. Smart (eds.), *o.c.*; N. Bala and R. Bromwich, *l.c.*

[58] C. Van Nijnatten, 'Authority Relations in Families and Child Welfare in The Netherlands and England: New Styles of Governance', *International Journal of Law, Policy, and the Family* 14, 2000, pp. 107–130.

[59] *E.g.*, M. Vonk, 'One, Two, or Three Parents? Lesbian Co-Mothers and a Known Donor with 'Family Life' Under Dutch Law', *International Journal of Law, Policy, and the Family* 18, 2004, pp. 103–117; B. Smyth, 'Parental-Child Contact in Australia: Exploring Five Different Post-Separation Patterns of Parenting', *International Journal of Law, Policy, and the Family* 19, 2005, pp. 1–22.

[60] A. Giddens, *Runaway World: How Global-ization is Reshaping Our Lives* (London, Profile Books, 1999).

[61] Anthony Giddens, *Runaway World: How Global-ization is Reshaping Our Lives* (London: Profile Books, 1999), at 12.

[62] *Ibid.*

27. With the exception of examinations of underage parenthood,[63] liberal relativist approaches have largely been adult-centred, focusing on the rights of 'parents' rather than on the child's rights. The dominance of adult-centred liberal approaches is, in general, explicable because most child rights perspectives have adopted liberal rather than dignified life or child rights-based perspectives. Archard, for example, commences his examination of child rights and childhood with a discussion of Locke.[64] Promisingly, certain child rights theorists and advocates, such as Freeman, have commendably advanced powerful moral and justice-based arguments to justify child rights.[65] The ideological tools employed however have emanated from dominant liberal rights theorists such as Dworkin and Rawls. As such, child rights theories have often been adult-centred and based on contract doctrine rather than social trust.

28. The exercises have often involved extrapolation of adult-based perspectives to child rights and children. Although approbating the CRC, Archard, for example, makes a stronger argument for parental rights than he does for the rights of children who are not yet adolescents, such as those who are a day old.[66] In contrast and commendably, Freeman notes the growing trend to focus on the child's rights to have contact with parents rather than merely on the parents' right to custody.[67] Eekelaar, reflecting the dominance of liberal thought, does not proffer the CRC's principles to resolve the lack of principle-based court decisions in situations of inter-cultural conflict regarding the upbringing of children. Instead, he offers a framework rooted in liberal theory: 'dynamic self-determinism', where autonomy limited by the need to prevent harm is a critical factor.[68] Burman has suggested a reconceptualization that recognizes local perspectives as interacting with global standards, to minimize cultural imperialism and moral relativism.[69]

---

[63] *E.g.*, H. Willekens, 'Rights and Duties of Underage Parents: A Comparative Approach', *International Journal of Law, Policy, and the Family* 18, 2004, pp. 355–370.

[64] D. Archard, *Children, Rights and Adulthood* (London Routledge, 2004).

[65] M. Freeman, 'The Limits of Children's Rights', in: M. Freeman and P. Veerman (eds.), *The Ideologies of Children's Rights* (London, Martinus Nijhoff Publishers), pp. 29–46; M. Freeman, 'Taking Children's Rights More Seriously', *International Journal of Law and the Family* 6, 1992, pp. 52–71; M. Freeman, *The Moral Status of Children: Essays on the Rights of the Child* (London, Martinus Nijhoff Publishers, 1997), especially chapters 1–5.

[66] D. Archard, *o.c.*, chapter 12.

[67] M. Freeman, *The Moral Status of Children: Essays on the Rights of the Child, o.c.*, chapter 8.

[68] J. Eekelaar, 'Children Between Cultures', *International Journal of Law and the Family* 18, 2004, pp. 178–194.

[69] E. Burman, 'Local, Global or Globalized? Child Development and International Child Rights Legislation', *Childhood: A Global Journal of Child Research* 3, No. 1, 1996, pp. 45–66.

However, whilst these contributions are practically useful, it is important to bear in mind that the object of decision-making and actions in a child rights-based approach is the dignified life of the child, and not the integrity of cultures.

29. In its favour, liberal relativism has helped question dominant ortho-dox perspectives on childhood and child-parent relationships. New albeit adult-centred liberal relativist approaches to the study of child develop-ment have rejected the 'idealisation of the stable two-parent nuclear fam-ily', as this 'fails to recognise the multiplicity of ways in which care can be provided.'[70] 'Western styles of child care' are thought by researchers such as Lansdown[71] to be incorporated into 'developmentally appropriate prac-tice' (DAP) as advocated by the US's National Association for the Education of Young Children.[72] However, it is easy to overplay the differences in care approaches. Both DAP and the alternative adult-centred liberal relativism rightly encourage responsiveness to social and cultural contexts. The alter-native adult centred-liberal relativism underlines 'contextually appropriate practice.'[73] On its part, DAP recognizes 'that children are best understood in the context of family, culture, and society.'[74] DAP is stronger however in stressing that children should reach 'their full potential in the context of relationships that are based on trust, respect, and positive regard.'[75] It is essential to underline though the importance of reflecting the principles of the CRC, a point buttressed even by Lansdown.[76] In this regard, Prout may be right to argue that just as there might be a diversity of childhoods, a common concept of childhood may be emerging.[77] Certainly the image of childhood in the CRC, based on child rights and child rights principles, is competing with other images. At the same time, the CRC-based image of childhood can claim trans-cultural acceptance, as evidenced by the near universal

---

[70] G. Lansdown, *The Evolving Capacities of the Child* (Florence; Save the Children and UNICEF, 2005), p. 18.

[71] *Ibid.*

[72] Association for the Education of Young Children, 'Developmentally Appropriate Practice in Early Childhood Programmes Serving Children from Birth through Age 8 (1996)', http://www.naeyc.org/about/positions/pdf/PSDAP98.PDF.

[73] M. Woodhead, *In search of the Rainbow: Pathways to Quality in Large scale Programmes for Young Disadvantaged Children* (The Hague, Bernard van Leer Foundation, 1996).

[74] Association for the Education of Young Children, *lc.*, pp. 4, 5 and 7.

[75] *Ibid.*, p. 4.

[76] G. Lansdown, *o.c.*, p. 19.

[77] A. Prout, *The Future of Childhood: Towards the Interdisciplinary Study of Children* (London/New York, Routledge Falmer, 2005).

ratification of the CRC. Hence, it is possible to agree with Freeman that the CRC requires the making of 'judgements across different communities'[78]

30. For six reasons, the obsession with 'families,' parenthood, and adult-centred liberal relativism may be misleading. Firstly, adult-centred liberal relativism may place harmful cultural or religious approaches before human rights. Such practices include female genital mutilation, child betrothal, and early marriages. Some of such practices have already been specified as challenges by certain regional standards.[79] The ACRWC requires States to 'eliminate harmful social and cultural practices affecting the welfare, dignity, normal growth and development of the child.'[80] The Charter particularizes 'customs and practices prejudicial to the health or life of the child'[81] and discriminatory practices, which exist in many African and other families.[82] It further requires States to prohibit child betrothal.[83] Direction and guidance that may result in the child being subjected to such practices is not compatible with the child rights principles and not "appropriate." These standards are not a reflection of 'cultural imperialism', but evidenced by facts that they are antithetical to the dignified life of the child.[84]

31. Secondly, adult-centred liberal relativism is questionable as a preferred trend in an increasingly interconnected and globalizing world that is in transformation. Appropriate direction and guidance is not the only source of influence for the child, in a world characterized by increasing proliferation and accessibility of information, information technologies, schools, and peers. The CRC includes an instrumental right to 'access information and material from a diversity of national and international sources, especially those aimed at the promotion of his or her social, spiritual and moral well-being and physical and mental health'.[85] At the same time, the CRC calls for the development of guidelines to protect the child from information that may be 'injurious to his or her well-being', bearing in mind the child's

---

[78] M. Freeman, 'Human Rights, Children's Rights and Judgement—Some Thoughts on Reconciling Universality and Pluralism', *The International Journal of Children's Rights* 10, 2002, pp. 345–354.

[79] *E.g.*, Article 21 of the ACRWC.

[80] Article 21(1) of the ACRWC.

[81] Article 21(1)(a) of the ACRWC.

[82] Article 21(1)(b) of the ACRWC; *e.g.* B. Rwezaura, 'The Value of a Child: Marginal Children and the Law in Contemporary Tanzania', *International Journal of Law, Policy and the Family* 14, 2000, pp. 326–364.

[83] Article 21(2) of the ACRWC.

[84] *E.g.*, UNICEF, *Early Marriage: A Harmful Traditional Practice* (Florence, UNICEF, 2005); UNICEF, *Female Genital Mutilation/Cutting* (New York, UNICEF, 2005).

[85] Article 17 of the CRC.

freedom of association and the role of parents in the upbringing of children.[86] In its Concluding Observations regarding Panama, for example, the CRC Committee urged the State Party to 'reinforce existing measures to protect children from harmful information.'[87]

32. Thirdly, whilst noting the changing and varying nature of families and parenthood, the CRC Committee[88] has doubted whether all forms of the family and parenthood are conducive to a CRC-based image of childhood. In certain cases, the Committee has expressed concern about the new forms of relationships and parenthood. It has accordingly asked countries to study the impact of such forms of parenthood and families. In this regard, the Committee has specified 'visiting' and 'common law relationships.'[89] The Committee has further expressed concern about the growing trend of single-parenthood, as it did with regard to Denmark.[90] A UNICEF study of child well-being in 21 rich countries partly concluded as follows:

> At the statistical level there is evidence to associate growing up in single-parent families and stepfamilies with greater risk to well-being—including a greater risk of dropping out of school, of leaving home early, of poorer health, of low skills, and of low pay. Furthermore such risks appear to persist even when the substantial effect of increased poverty levels in single-parent and stepfamilies have been taken into account.[91]

33. Whilst some of such forms of families or parenthood may be freely chosen by adults, others in poor or conflict-ridden countries arise as a result of vulnerability. Thus the CRC Committee has required State Parties such as Burundi to 'give particular attention to the establishment of psycho-social and parental guidance programmes to strengthen vulnerable family units such as single-parent-, child- and grandparent-headed households.'[92]

---

[86] *Ibid.*

[87] CRC Committee, *Concluding Observations: Panama* (UN Doc. CRC/C/15/Add.68, 1997), para. 30.

[88] CRC Committee, *Day of General Discussion on the Role of the Family in the Promotion of the Rights of the Child* (UN Doc. CRC/C/24, 1994)

[89] *E.g.*, CRC Committee, *Concluding Observations: Grenada* (UN Doc. CRC/C/15/Add.121, 2000), para. 17; *Saint Kitts and Nevis* (UN Doc. CRC/C/15/Add.104, 1999), paras. 21 and 22.

[90] CRC Committee, *Concluding Observations: Denmark* (UN Doc. CRC/C/15/Add.151, 2001), paras. 32 and 33.

[91] UNICEF, *Child Poverty in Perspective: An Overview of Child Well-being in Rich Countries* (Florence, UNICEF, 2007), pp. 23–24.

[92] CRC Committee, *Concluding Observations: Burundi* (UN Doc. CRC/C/15/Add.133, 2000), paras. 46 and 47.

34. Fourthly, international and regional tribunals have underlined that parental wishes must be overridden if harm may result against the health, development, and in general, well-being of the child. Parental wishes have, for example, been overridden in cases of child sexual abuse.[93] Parental wishes that a child should not participate in a school parade were overridden even though the parents thought that to guide the child otherwise would be in line with their rights to religion and family life.[94] Similarly, blood transfusion has been ordered for children in jurisdictions such as New Zealand, despite parental protestations.[95] In the United Kingdom, the clear advantage to test a child for HIV has outweighed parental wishes.[96]

35. Fifthly, whilst Article 5 of the CRC is very much about parents and other key carers, it does not focus on families. Instead, the Article refers to 'members of the extended family or community.' The correlative duties to the child's rights are hence not on families or communities. Instead, the duties are on individuals who may belong to the relevant social units. This interpretation would also justify court decisions that have upheld the rights of grandparents to bring up or have contact with a child, subject to the best interests of the child.[97] The logic of the approach in a globalizing world is exemplified by increasing recognition of legal and moral roles for community members regarding the upbringing of a child. In the United Kingdom, the introduction of anti-social behaviour orders extends the hitherto supposed 'triangular' relationship between the state, the family and the child.[98] That relationship is increasingly recognized to include communities as well. Jack has argued persuasively that recent legislation in the United Kingdom

---

[93] *E.g.*, Human Rights Committee, *Clarence T. Maloney* v. *Germany*, Communication No. 755/1997, 15 March 1996, (UN Doc. CCPR/C/60/D/755/1997, 1997).

[94] ECtHR, *Efstratiou* v. *Greece*, 18 December 1996, *Reports*, 1996–VI.

[95] *Re J (An Infant) B and B v Director-General of Social Welfare* [1996] *2 New Zealand Law Reports*, 134, (New Zealand Court of Appeal, 3rd April, 1996

[96] In Re C (A Child) (HIV Test) [1999] *2 Family Law Reports* 1004, England and Wales Court of Appeal, 21st September, 1999.

[97] F. Kaganas and C. Piper, 'Grandparents and Contact: 'Rights v Welfare' Revisited', *International Journal of Law, Policy, and the Family* 15, 2001, pp. 250–275; T.L. Henderson, 'Grandparent Visitation Rights: Successful Acquisition of Court-Ordered Visitation', *Journal of Family Issues* 26, No. 1, 2005, pp. 107–137; T.L. Henderson, 'Grandparents Visitation Rights: Justices' Interpretation of the Best Interest of the Child Standard', *Journal of Family Issues* 26, No. 5, 2005, pp. 638–664 (2005).

[98] A. Cleland and K. Tisdal, 'The Challenge of Antisocial Behaviour: The New Relationships Between the State, Children and Parents', *International Journal of Law, Policy, and the Family* 19, 2005, pp. 395–420.

requires greater consideration of the 'area and community components' of child well-being in the delivery of services.[99]

36. Sixthly, parents are not the only persons mentioned in Article 5. The Article refers to 'parents or, where applicable, the members of the extended family or community as provided for by local custom, legal guardians or other persons legally responsible for the child.' The inclusion of 'other persons legally responsible for the child' provides the genus of those that have the correlative duty to the child's right at the household and community levels or similar contexts. The implication is that the list is not closed, as long as the person is 'legally responsible for the child.' In all country reports so far considered by the CRC Committee, State Parties have always indicated that their respective laws specify parents as those primarily responsible for their children.[100] One key reason for this position has long been presented as a natural and moral convergence of biological and reproductive consequences, as articulated by Schouler as early as 1870. Schouler argued that 'it is a plain precept of universal law that young and tender beings

---

[99] G. Jack, 'The Area and Community Components of Children's Well-being', *Children & Society* 20, 2006, pp. 334–347.

[100] *E.g.*, UN Committee on the Rights of the Child (CRC), *UN Committee on the Rights of the Child: State Party Report*: Barbados. 11/02/97, CRC/C/3/Add.45), para. 72; UN Committee on the Rights of the Child (CRC), *UN Committee on the Rights of the Child: State Party Report*: Belgium. 06/09/94. CRC/C/11/Add.4), 160; UN Committee on the Rights of the Child (CRC), *UN Committee on the Rights of the Child: State Party Report*: Benin. 04/07/97; CRC/C/3/Add.52, para. 107; UN Committee on the Rights of the Child (CRC), *UN Committee on the Rights of the Child: State Party Report*: Bulgaria. 12/10/95; CRC/C/8/Add.29, para. 92; UN Committee on the Rights of the Child (CRC), *UN Committee on the Rights of the Child: State Party Report*: China. 01/08/95; CRC/C/11/Add.7, para. 80; UN Committee on the Rights of the Child (CRC), *UN Committee on the Rights of the Child: State Party Report*: Croatia. 07/12/94, CRC/C/8/Add.19, para. 188; UN Committee on the Rights of the Child (CRC), *UN Committee on the Rights of the Child: State Party Report*: Czech Republic. 17/06/96; CRC/C/11/Add.11, para. 80; UN Committee on the Rights of the Child (CRC), *UN Committee on the Rights of the Child: State Party Report*: Democratic People's Republic of Korea. 17/06/96; CRC/C/3/Add.41, para. 90–91; UN Committee on the Rights of the Child (CRC), *UN Committee on the Rights of the Child: State Party Report*: Libyan Arab Jamahiriya 26/09/96; CRC/C/28/Add.6, para. 71; UN Committee on the Rights of the Child (CRC), *UN Committee on the Rights of the Child: State Party Report*: Panama. 28/09/95; CRC/C/8/Add.28. paras. 101–102; UN Committee on the Rights of the Child (CRC), *UN Committee on the Rights of the Child: State Party Report*: Peru. 10/11/92; CRC/C/3/Add.7, para. 50; UN Committee on the Rights of the Child (CRC), *UN Committee on the Rights of the Child: State Party Report*: Russian Federation. 22/10/92; CRC/C/3/Add.5, para. 90; UN Committee on the Rights of the Child (CRC), *UN Committee on the Rights of the Child: State Party Report*: South Africa. 22/05/99; CRC/C/51/Add.2, paras. 292–293; UN Committee on the Rights of the Child (CRC), *UN Committee on the Rights of the Child: State Party Report*: United Kingdom of Great Britain and Northern Ireland. 28/03/94; CRC/C/11/Add.1, para. 199; UN Committee on the Rights of the Child (CRC), *UN Committee on the Rights of the Child: State Party Report*: Venezuela. 22/09/97; CRC/C/3/Add.54, para. 105—all accessible at http://www.unhchr.ch/tbs/doc.nsf.

should be nurtured and brought up by parents.'[101] By begetting children, Schouler argued, parents enter 'into voluntary obligations to endeavour as far as in them lies, that the life which they have bestowed shall be supported and preserved.'[102]

37. The direction and guidance the parents and other carers have to provide to the child has to be consistent with a CRC-based image of childhood. The child is hence not just an object to be guided and directed, but a person who is entitled to parental and other carers' direction and guidance. Semantically, 'guidance' and 'direction' are related. 'Direction' however entails a way and the existence of purpose. 'Guidance' entails supervision, assistance and instructions in the process of proceeding in a direction. Taken together, as Article 5 of the CRC does, the point is that a child's life must be purposeful.

38. The child's right to appropriate direction and guidance applies to the exercise of all the rights recognized in the Convention. In this regard, it is surprising that the Article was not identified by the CRC Committee as containing a principle for the Convention.[103] Work by Lansdown under UNICEF's Innocenti Research Centre sponsorship, in contrast, strongly presents Article 5 of the CRC as containing a principle for the realisation of child rights.[104]

39. It is easy though to suppose that since the word 'exercise' has conventionally been associated with civil liberties, then the Article pertains only to those provisions that enshrine civil liberties. Three of the Articles describing civil liberties spell limitations or restrictions in the enjoyment of the child's human rights.[105] The enjoyment of freedom of expression is subject to the rights and reputations of other people.[106] The freedoms of thought, conscience, and religion are subject to the protection of 'public safety, order (*ordre public*), health or public morals, or the fundamental rights and freedoms of others.'[107] The guidance with regard to the exercise of the freedom

---

[101] J. Schouler, *A Treatise on the Law of Domestic Relations: Embracing Husband and Wife, Parent and Child, Guardian and Ward, Infancy, and Master and Servant* (Boston, Little Brown, 1870), p. 366.

[102] *Ibid.*, p. 367.

[103] CRC Committee, *General Guidelines Regarding the Form and Content of Initial Reports to be Submitted by States Parties under Article 44, Paragraph 1(a), of the Convention, o.c.*

[104] G. Lansdown, *o.c.*

[105] Articles 13, 14 and 15 of the CRC.

[106] Article 13(2) of the CRC.

[107] Article 14(3) of the CRC.

of association has to ensure the protection of democracy, national security or public safety, public order, public health and 'the rights and freedoms of others.'[108] However, even in the case of civil liberties, the word 'exercise' means 'to make use.' There is no sense then that can prevent the child's right to receive appropriate direction and guidance from applying to the economic, social and cultural rights in the Convention.

3.2   Rights Holders and Duty Bearers

40. According to Article 5 of the CRC, the duty to provide direction and guidance to the child is on parents and other key carers. Alston's view,[109] endorsed by Detrick,[110] is that the Article is not a comprehensive recognition of duties and responsibilities of parents and carers. Alston thinks that the Article does not prescribe any duty. The reason he gives is that an international convention can only impose duties on its State Parties.[111] This Statist perspective is incorrect. Firstly, Article 5 of the CRC prescribes at least one duty for parents and carers: the duty to provide 'appropriate direction and guidance in the exercise' of the child's rights. Secondly, the orthodox view that international law is solely about States has been challenged by the dynamics of globalization, as civil society, corporations, and individuals increasingly become actors in both the formation and implementation of international law and global governance.[112] Van Bueren's examination of the international law on child rights cites numerous examples of provisions that recognize non-state actors as subjects and addressees of international law.[113] From the perspective of dignified life, there is no reason to prevent the CRC from 'imposing' or indicating duties upon parents and other actors.

---

[108] Article 15(2) of the CRC.
[109] P. Alston, l.c., p. 13.
[110] S. Detrick, o.c., pp. 119–120.
[111] P. Alston, l.c., pp. 13–14.
[112] E.g., B. Rajagopal, *International Law from Below: Development, Social Movements and Third World Resistance* (Cambridge, Cambridge University Press, 2003); B. de Sousa Santos and C.A. Rodríguez-Garavito, *Law and Globalization from Below: Towards a Cosmopolitan Legality* (Cambridge, Cambridge University Press, 2005).
[113] G. Van Bueren, *The International Law of Child Rights* (The Hague, Kluwer Law International, 1998), chapter 3; G. Van Bueren, 'The International Protection of Family Members' Rights as the 21st Century Approaches', l.c., pp. 732–765.

41. Article 5 of the CRC, in fact, imposes duties on other actors who may be involved in the upbringing of the child, in addition to parents and other primary carers and the State. The scope of duty bearers in the Article includes 'where applicable, the members of the extended family or community as provided for by local custom, legal guardians or other persons legally responsible for the child.' This scope of duty bearers encapsulates all legal primary care givers. Such legality may emanate from State law or custom, according to the Article. However, analyses of the Article's *travaux préparatoires* have suggested that the reference to members of the extended family was to cater for situations 'when' there were no parents.[114] Such carers are, of course, logically encapsulated by the Article. It is important nevertheless to notice that the Article uses the phrase 'where applicable' and not 'when applicable'. The semantic difference entails that the reference to extended family members cannot be limited to situations where the child has no parents. Rather, members of extended families are duty bearers for the child's right, where local custom provides so. This would cater for numerous situations in Africa and other societies of the South, where extended family members play crucial roles in the provisions of direction and guidance to children.[115] Such roles, captured by the phrase 'responsibilities, rights, and duties', are notably growing in number and burden, as incidents of orphanhood increase in Sub-Saharan Africa significantly due to AIDS.[116]

42. Previous commentaries have not elaborated on the jurisprudential differences between 'responsibilities', 'rights', and 'duties' in relation to the general correlative duty on the part of key care givers. The common aspect among these three terms is the signification of the *roles* that parents and other key carers have to realize in the context of the child's right to receive parental guidance. The Article's use of all the three words indicates its spirit to be as encompassing as possible in ensuring that those who have parental and similar key care *roles* to the child provide appropriate guidance to the child. Various jurisdictions seem to relate both 'right' and 'duty' conjunctively when referring to the roles of parents and other key carers. Rwanda, Romania, Portugal, Peru, Slovenia, Azerbaijan, Bulgaria, Croatia, Ghana, Eritrea, Estonia, Germany, Italy, Kyrgyzstan, Lithuania, Macedonia, Senegal,

---

[114] *E.g.*, S. Detrick, *A Commentary on the United Nations Convention on the Rights of the Child, o.c.*, p. 119.

[115] G. Van Bueren, *The International Law of Child Rights, o.c.*, pp. 68–69.

[116] UNAIDS, UNICEF, and USAID, *Children on the Brink 2004: A Joint Report of New Orphan Estimates and a Framework for Action* (New York, UNAIDS/UNICEF/USAID, 2004).

Uganda, and Paraguay[117] all indicate that parents have the right and duty regarding the care, upbringing, instruction, or support of their children.

43. Article 5 of the CRC's reference to 'responsibility' is important because it captures all those decisions and actions expected for those in the roles of parents, guardians, community and extended families, and others who may be in such or similar relationships with the child as provided by law or local custom. The CRC does not define the term responsibility. However, a Council of Europe Recommendation is instructive on the meaning of parental responsibility. For the purposes of that Recommendation,

> parental responsibilities are a collection of duties and powers which aim at ensuring the moral and material welfare of the child, in particular by taking care of the person of the child, by maintaining personal relationships with him and by providing for his education, his maintenance, his legal representation and the administration of his property.[118]

44. This is similar to the definition of parental responsibility in the Children Act 1989 of England and Wales. That Act describes parental responsibility as 'all the rights, duties, powers, responsibilities and authority which by law a parent of a child has in relation to the child and his [or her] property.'[119] The CRC has examples of roles entailed by use of the term 'responsibility.' It provides that parents 'or, as the case may be, legal guardians, have the primary responsibility for the upbringing and development of the child.'[120] The primary responsibility to secure 'the conditions of living necessary for child's development' lie with parents and others 'responsible for the child', 'within their abilities and financial capacities.'[121] The CRC further takes it for

---

[117] Article 24(2) of the Constitution of Rwanda (1991); Article 48(2) of the Constitution of Romania (1991); Article 26(5) of the Constitution of Portugal (1976); Article 6 of the Constitution of Peru (1993); Article 54 of the Constitution of Slovenia (1991); Article 34 of the Constitution of Azerbaijan (1995); Article 47 of the Constitution of Bulgaria (1991); Article 63(2) of the Constitution of Croatia (1990); Section 28(1)(c) of the Constitution of Ghana (1996); Article 22(3) of the Constitution of Eritrea (1996); Article 27(3) of the Constitution of Estonia (1992); Article 6(2) of the Constitution of Germany (1949); Article 30(1) of the Constitution of Italy (1947); Article 26(1) of the Constitution of Kyrgyzstan (1993); Article 38 of the Constitution of Lithuania (1992); Article 40 of the Constitution of the Former Yugoslav Republic of Macedonia (1991); Article 20 of the Constitution of Senegal (2001); Article 31(4) of the Constitution of Uganda (1995); Article 53(1) of the Constitution of Paraguay (1992). All are accessible through http://confinder.richmond.edu/.

[118] Council of Europe, Committee of Ministers, Recommendation No. R(84)4 of the Committee of Ministers to Member States on Parental Responsibilities, o.c., Principle 1.

[119] Chapter 41, Article 3(1) of the Children Act (1989) (C.41 of the Laws of England and Wales).

[120] Article 18(1) of the CRC.

[121] Article 27(2) of the CRC.

granted that there should be people who have the responsibility for 'main-tenance' [122] and 'financial' responsibility[123] of the child. The ACRWC further provides an example of a responsibility for parents and other key carers. Such people, the Charter stipulates, 'have the primary responsibility of the upbringing and development the child.'[124] Croatia's Constitution illustra-tively states that parents are 'responsible for ensuring the rights of their children to harmonious development of their personalities.'[125] Similarly, Estonia's Constitution prescribes that parents have the 'responsibility for the raising and care of their children.'[126] In Mozambique, the law is that the family is 'responsible for raising children in a harmonious manner.'[127]

45. Comparatively, Article 5 of the CRC's use of the term 'duties' refers to parental or similar obligations that are correlative to the child's rights, in general and in response to specific situations. The State is correlatively the principle duty bearer, being the main addressee of the Convention. In this regard, international law jurisprudence pertaining to duties correlative to human rights has, through General Comments, helpfully provided a cate-gorisation of obligations for States and others. There are four types of obli-gations for the State. These are obligations to respect, protect, promote, and fulfil the enjoyment of particular human rights.[128] Importantly, the State's obligations are to the child and the child's key care givers.

46. Firstly, the duty to respect, specifically mentioned in Article 5 of the CRC, entails non-interference with and non-violation of rights. The State is required to respect the role of parents and other key carers as primary duty bearers. The provision for this duty allows the exercise of parental roles in the upbringing of children. To the parents and other key carers, the general duty for the State is to respect these carers' rights, duties, and responsibili-ties. As a principal duty bearer, the State must ensure that there is clarity on the nature and scope of those rights, duties, and responsibilities. The State then should not interfere with the exercise of such rights and the discharge

---

[122] Article 26(2) of the CRC.
[123] Article 27(4) of the CRC.
[124] Article 20(1) of the ACRWC.
[125] Article 63(2) of the Constitution of Croatia (1990), accessible through http://confinder.richmond.edu/.
[126] Article 27(3) of the Constitution of Estonia (1992), accessible through http://confinder.richmond.edu/.
[127] Article 120(2) of the Constitution of Mozambique (1999), accessible through http://confinder.richmond.edu/.
[128] *E.g.*, CESCR Committee, *General Comment No. 3. The Nature of States Parties' Obligations* (UN Doc. HRI/GEN/1/Rev.7, 1990).

of the duties except to ensure the best interests of the child and compliance with other child rights principles. Certain countries have constitutionally recognized the right of parents to bring up and instruct their children, exemplified by Poland's Constitution in the following terms:

> Parents shall have the right to rear their children in accordance with their own convictions. Such upbringing shall respect the degree of maturity of a child as well as his freedom of conscience and belief and also his convictions.[129]

47. Similarly, Ireland's Constitution, stipulates that the State 'acknowledges' the family as a 'primary and natural educator of the child.' Consequently, the Irish State is expected to 'respect the inalienable right and duty of parents to provide, according to their means, for the religious and moral, intellectual, physical and social education of their children.'[130] In the European legal system, the state's wrongful interference with parental roles has successfully been challenged, albeit often linked to the protection of the right to family life.[131] Analysed, such cases have been successful largely because there have not been threats to the well-being and best interests of the child. Indeed, in *Hendricks v Netherlands*, the European Commission on Human Rights described the child's interests as 'overriding.'[132]

48. For the child, the State's duty is to respect the right to receive appropriate direction and guidance, according to her or his evolving capacities. This, however, has hitherto been a much unrecognized right, despite its enshrinement in the CRC's Article 5. Not only have previous commentaries not expressly identified this right, but jurisdictions are yet to accord it explicit recognition, at least at the constitutional level. However, references to duties on parents and key carers in certain constitutions entail recognition, correlatively, of the child's right to parental guidance.

49. Secondly, the State's duty to protect entails proactive preventive and responsive measures for the child when the right to parental guidance is at risk. A State's blanket refraining from interference with the exercise of parental roles may not necessarily result in appropriate direction and

---

[129] Article 48(1) of the Constitution of Poland (1997), accessible through http://confinder.richmond.edu/.

[130] Article 42(1) of the Constitution of Ireland (1937), accessible through http://confinder.richmond.edu/. Also *cf. supra.*

[131] *E.g.,* ECtHR, *O v. United Kingdom*, 8 July 1987, *Publications of the Court*, Series A, 121; *Olsson v. Sweden (No. 1)*, 24 March 1988, *Publications of the Court*, Series A, 130; *Margareta and Roger Andersson v. Sweden*, 25 February 1992, *Publications of the Court*, Series A, 226-A.

[132] European Commission on Human Rights, *Hendricks v. Netherlands*, (1983) 5 EHRR 223, decided in 1983.

guidance. Blanket autonomy for parents and other carers may also not result in appropriate direction and guidance. Similarly, there is no guarantee that parental guidance will be exercised in a manner that recognizes the child's evolving capacities, if there is blanket autonomy. Further, the exercise or neglect of appropriate direction and guidance for the child may result in the physical, emotional, sexual, or other abuse of the child. In situations of abuse and neglect, the CRC is clear that the State must intervene to protect the enjoyment of the rights of the child for the child's progressive well-being or dignified life.[133] State Parties and State agencies have hence been justified to take a child into care, away from abusive or neglectful parents or key duty bearers.[134] On the other hand, the damning evidence of world-wide abuse and neglect of children demonstrates the general failure on part of States to protect the child's right to appropriate direction and guidance.[135] In addition to abuse and neglect in school and educational settings, care and justice institutions, places of work and communities, the home and family settings represent the paradox of care and abuse and neglect and discrimination with regard to the child's dignified life. In the words of the World Report on Violence against Children:

> In the home and family setting, children experience assaults and other acts of physical violence, sexual violation, harmful traditional practices, humiliation and other types of psychological violence, and neglect. As well as assaults and other physical violence, these can include acts of omission, such as failure to protect the child from exposure to preventable violence at the hands of friends, neighbours, or visitors; acts of stigma or gross discrimination; and failure to utilize child health and welfare services to support the child's well-being. Perpetrators of violence in the home circle include parents and step-parents, and can also include alternative family carers, extended family, spouses (in the case of child marriage) and their in-laws.[136]

50. Thirdly, the duty to promote the child's right to appropriate direction and guidance entails raising awareness and understanding regarding the nature, scope, and implications of the right. This duty to promote the child's right to appropriate direction and guidance is hence linked to the measures of implementation of child rights, required by the CRC's Article 4(1) and the

---

[133] Articles 19, 34 and 36 of the CRC.

[134] *E.g.*, ECtHR, *Margareta and Roger Andersson v Sweden*, l.c.

[135] P.S. Pinheiro, Independent Expert for the United Nations, Secretary-General's Study on Violence against Children, *World Report on Violence against Children* (Geneva; OHCHR, UNICEF, WHO, 2006); also: United Nations, *Report of the Independent Expert for the United Nations Study on Violence Against Children*, 29 August 2006, http://www.violencestudy.org/IMG/pdf/English-2-2.pdf.

[136] P.S. Pinheiro, *o.c.*, pp. 50–51.

related General Comment.[137] The CRC Committee has proposed to States to implement parental education programmes that would involve knowledge and understanding of child rights.[138] In the case of Brunei Durra Salaam, the CRC Committee noted the provision of a premarital course in the country and urged the State Party to infuse child rights principles in that curriculum.[139]

51. Fourthly, the State's duty to fulfil the child's appropriate direction and guidance is twofold. The first entails the duty to provide for the enjoyment of the right. In this regard, Concluding Observations by the Committee on the Rights of the Child have been instructive. The Committee has urged States to provide parental education and support to parents in need. This guidance underlines the importance of optimum capacity in terms of human, economic, and organisational resources for the enjoyment of the child's right. The second prong of the duty to fulfil the child's right to appropriate direction and guidance is to facilitate enjoyment. This means that the State has to ensure that a conducive environment exists for the prevalence of appropriate parental guidance and direction. This may require support and approbation to civil society organizations that are able to provide parental education. It also entails the facilitation of the proper performance of duties at all levels, which would result in the enjoyment of the child's right to direction and guidance.

52. The State is not the only duty bearer for the child's right to direction and guidance. In addition to Article 5, the CRC's Articles 3 and 14 assume that there should be people in society who have duties for the progressive dignified life or well-being of the child. Article 5 joins Article 18 to recognize parents and other key duty bearers as primary duty bearers for the enjoyment of the child's rights. Usefully, the ACRWC provides examples of broad duties for parents and other key carers in the following terms:[140]

    (a) to ensure that the best interests of the child are their basic concern at all times;

---

[137] CRC Committee, *General Comment No. 5. General Measures of Implementation of the Convention on the Rights of the Child* (UN Doc. CRC/GC/2003/5, 2003), Arts. 4, 42 and 44, para. 6

[138] *E.g.*, CRC Committee, *Concluding Observations: Bulgaria* (UN Doc. CRC/C/15/Add.66, 1997), para. 28; *Panama* (UN Doc. CRC/C/15/Add.68, 1997), para. 30; *Sierra Leone* (UN Doc. CRC/C/15/Add.116, 2000), para. 49; *Oman* (UN Doc. CRC/C/OMN/CO/2, 2006), para. 37; *Saint Lucia* (UN Doc. CRC/C/15/Add.258, 2005), para. 37.

[139] CRC Committee, *Concluding observations: Brunei Darussalam* (UN Doc. CRC/C/15/Add.219, 2003), para. 40.

[140] Article 20(1)(a-c) of the ACRWC.

(b) to secure, within their abilities and financial capacities, conditions of living necessary to the child's development; and

(c) to ensure that domestic discipline is administered with humanity and in a manner consistent with the inherent dignity of the child.

53. These examples are useful for the interpretation and application of the CRC's Article 5. The duties underlined in the ACRWC's Article 20, if breached, entail that the State should intervene to protect the child's rights. Examples of such intervention include the banning in certain countries of physical punishment as a form of child discipline. Swedish law, for example, has long banned the physical punishment of children both within and outside the home.[141] The CRC Committee is encouraging other countries to do likewise.[142]

54. In contrast to 'duty', the use of the term 'right' signifies a legal or moral entitlement or claim to decisions and actions for people *in loco parentis* as against other actors. On this premise, a call to replace 'the rights ethic' with a 'care ethic' to adopt a needs-based approach is contrary to the logic of the CRC.[143] The CRC's ethic is for a child rights-based approach that respects the child as a holder of rights. In other words, the right referred to in Article 5 of the CRC pertains to claims that parents and other key carers should have in providing appropriate direction and guidance. Included are rights that are instrumental for the provision of parental guidance, such as the right to reside with the child, traditionally misrepresented as custody of the child.[144] The correlative duty bearers to such rights are those who must respect the role of a parent or other key carer to provide appropriate guidance to the

---

[141] Parents, Guardians and Children Code, SFS 1983:485, Chapter 6, http://www.sweden .gov.se/content/1/c6/02/76/55/12308db5.pdf s. 3. Also, Swedish Government, *Can You Bring Up Children Successfully Without Smacking and Spanking?* (Stockholm, Ministry of Justice); J. Durrant, 'Legal Reform and Attitudes Toward Physical Punishment in Sweden', *The International Journal of Children's Rights* 11, 2003, pp. 147–173.

[142] CRC Committee, *General Comment No. 8. The Right of the Child to Protection from Corporal Punishment and Other Cruel or Degrading Forms of Punishment (Arts. 19; 28, para. 2; and 37, inter alia)* (UN Doc. CRC/C/GC/8, 2006).

[143] *E.g.*, T. Cockburn, 'Children and the Feminist Ethic of Care', *Childhood: A Global Journal of Child Research* 12, No, 1, 2005, pp. 71–89; F. Kelly, 'Conceptualising the Child Through an 'Ethic of Care': Lessons for Family Law', *International Journal of Law in Context* 1, No. 4, 2005, pp. 375–396.

[144] *E.g.*, India, *Githa Hariharan & Anor v Reserve Bank of India & Anor and Another Writ Petition* [1999] 1 LRI 353, (1999) 2 CHRLD 199, (1999) 2 SCC 228, (Supreme Court of India), decided on 17 February, 1999; Bangladesh, *Abdul Jalil & Ors v Sharon Laily Begum* 50 DLR (AD) (1998) 55, decided on 30 May 2001; South Africa, *LS v AT & Anor* 2001 (2) BCLR 152, (Constitutional Court, decided on 4 December, 2000); Fiji Islands: *Surya Prakash v Shirley Reshmi Narayan* Civil Appeal No. HBA0001J.99L, unreported, High Court, decided on 5 May, 2000; Mauritius: *Jordan v Jordan & Ors* Record No 66135, unreported, High Court, 29 February, 2000.

child. The Article gives the example of the State, but there are many at all levels of society who must respect parental and similar roles.

55. The reference to 'duties' in Article 5 of the CRC to the child's right to appropriate direction and guidance on part of the State and other duty bearers entails accountability. Duty bearers are accountable and can be held responsible for the performance of their duties or the perpetration of negative roles. On their part, rights holders and duty bearers at lower levels as rights holders have to demand the enjoyment of their rights. The obligation to facilitate such possibility and facilities lies on the State, the principle duty bearer in the Convention. It is civil society that has historically and potentially the most effective role to facilitate accountability. Through advocatory strategies,[145] response to State failures in the provisions of services, and capacity development for rights holders at all societal levels, civil society plays potentially an instrumental role in the realization of Article 5 of the CRC. In this connection, the Article's emphasis on the need to recognize the child's evolving capacities underscores the child's participation in a process of accountability for her or his progressive dignified life. The possible polarisation of relations between the child and her or his carers in such a situation is minimized by the Article's placement of duties on the State to ensure parental direction and guidance is appropriate.[146]

56. The State, however, as a duty bearer, needs to have the requisite capacity to ensure and facilitate provision of appropriate direction and guidance. In this regard, Article 5 must be read with Article 4 of the CRC. Article 4 makes the State a rights holder entitled to international cooperation, at least with regard to economic, social, and cultural rights. In this sense, the child is not the only rights holder logically envisaged in Article 5. The State is a rights holder, in the context of international cooperation, in the execution of its duties to respect, protect, promote, and fulfil for the realisation of the child's right. The dominant reality, since the adoption of the Convention, however, is that international cooperation to realize human rights is more based on charity than a rights paradigm. The duty to cooperate to ensure development is yet to be expressly effectuated by binding modalities that would ensure compliance on part of States, irrespective of the hopes that may be raised by the Declaration on the Right to Development.[147] That Declaration,

---

[145] U. Beck, *Power in the Global Age* (Cambridge, Polity Press, 2005), Chapter 6, pp. 236–248.

[146] *E.g.*, Article 19, in addition to Article 5 of the CRC.

[147] United Nations, Declaration on the Right to Development, adopted by the General Assembly on 4 December 1986, G.A. res. 41/128 (UN Doc. A/41/53, 1986).

in fact, embodies international law's hesitancy on the point, attempting to mix duties for States and respect for sovereignty in international cooperation. The duty to cooperate, according to the Declaration, has to be 'in such a manner as to promote a new international economic order.'[148] That new economic order has to be 'based on sovereign equality, interdependence, mutual interest and co-operation among all States, as well as to encourage the observance and realization of human rights.'[149]

57. For the effectuation of the Article, the State and the child are not the only logically recognized rights holders. Just as the State has to have requisite capacity to perform its duties, so too the parents, guardians, and where applicable, members of extended families and communities. In this connection, the CRC Committee has expressed this concern:

> The Committee is concerned that insufficient account is taken of the resources, skills and personal commitment required of parents and others responsible for young children, especially in societies where early marriage and parenthood is still sanctioned as well as in societies with a high incidence of young, single parents.[150]

58. In other words, State Parties have an obligation to ensure that all parents and other primary care providers have the requisite capacities to provide appropriate direction and guidance to the child. There are two significations for this duty. The first is that the State has to understand the capacity strengths and gaps of parents and other primary carers for children. Thus the CRC Committee has sometimes recommended studies on the issue, such as on the impact of 'visiting' relationships for countries such as Saint Kitts and Nevis.[151] The second signification is that the State has primary duties to address the manifestations and causes of lack of or inappropriate direction and guidance, consistent with the child's evolving capacities. In any given environment, the causes for inappropriate provision of parental guidance have a synergy of causes that require careful assessment, analysis, and a holistic response. Causes that have aroused concern for the CRC Committee have to be addressed, responsive to the social contexts. So far identified

---

[148] *Ibid.*

[149] *Ibid.*, Article 3(2).

[150] CRC Committee, *General Comment No. 7. Implementing Child Rights in Early Childhood*, o.c., para. 20.

[151] CRC Committee, *Concluding Observations: Saint Kitts and Nevis* (UN Doc. CRC/C/15/Add. 104, 1999).

by the CRC Committee have been early marriages and parenthood,[152] single parenthood,[153] parental separation,[154] separation from parents,[155] child abuse within households,[156] increasing incidents of orphanhood,[157] neglect, abandonment, and deprivation of parental care.[158]

59. The CRC Committee's recommendation, in the case of early childhood development, is instructive. The Committee advocates the development of 'rights-based, coordinated, multisectoral strategies in order to ensure that children's best interests are always a starting point for service planning and provision.'[159]

60. The CRC Committee has given indications of the measures that the State has to undertake to contribute to the capacity development of parents and other carers. The State has to provide parental education, parental guidance and counselling, support single parent families, and establish and facilitate child guidance schemes. The State could also consider the provision of pre-marital courses to prospective parents.[160] Such measures are matters of duty, not charity. The cogent implication is that parents and other primary carers are rights holders for the child's right to receive appropriate direction and guidance.

3.3 The Intended Results of Direction and Guidance

61. Article 5 of the CRC has a two-pronged purpose that must guide the intended results of respecting, protecting, promoting and fulfilling the enjoyment of the right to receive appropriate direction and guidance. The first is the exercise of child rights by the child. The second prong is the availability of appropriate direction and guidance.

---

[152] CRC Committee, *General Comment No. 8. The Right of the Child to Protection from Corporal Punishment and Other Cruel or Degrading Forms of Punishment (Arts. 19; 28, para. 2; and 37, inter alia)*, o.c.

[153] *Ibid.*

[154] *Ibid.*

[155] *Ibid.*

[156] CRC Committee, *General Comment No. 4. Adolescent Health and Development in the Context of the Convention on the Rights of the Child* (UN Doc. CRC/GC/2003/4, 2003), paras. 12 and 16.

[157] CRC Committee, *General Comment No. 3. HIV/AIDS and the Right of the Child* (UN Doc. CRC/GC/2003/3, 2003).

[158] CRC Committee, *General Comment No. 7. Implementing Child Rights in Early Childhood, o.c.,* para. 24.

[159] *Ibid.,* para. 22.

[160] *Ibid.*

62. Article 5 reflects the three principal reasons for special human rights for children or child rights, such as those stipulated in the CRC. Firstly, such human rights are necessary because children are vulnerable and, to a significant extent, dependent on close relationships. The CRC Committee observes, reflecting Article 5 of the CRC, that such 'relationships are normally with a small number of key people, most often parents, members of the extended family and peers, as well as caregivers.'[161] Secondly, children are future adults. As human beings, children evolve into adulthood. Their capacities develop subject to the care, environment, and direction and guidance that they receive. In this sense, the principle of the child's evolving capacities, embedded in Article 5, is crucial not only to current individual children, but also to the stature of future societies, parents, and children. Thirdly, child rights are necessary because they are about fairness within and between generations, or, intra-and inter-generational equity. The logic of human rights insists that since children are human beings, they must enjoy their human rights, to cater for their human needs as children and future adults. In this sense, Article 5 underlines that the appropriate direction and guidance must be connected to the exercise or enjoyment of her or his human rights, as enshrined in the CRC.

63. The child's exercise of her or his rights is the other prong in the Article's purpose. Appropriate direction and guidance must result in the exercise of child rights, with the child increasingly using her or his evolving capacities as she or he inter-depends with parents and other key carers. The exercise of rights, however, is necessary to achieve at least four broad human goals that are particularly pertinent for children. Those goals have also been identified by many as the broad objectives for child rights.[162] The first is the child's survival. The second is that as the child survives, she or he must enjoy optimal development. The third is that as she or he develops, she or he must participate in matters that may affect her or him. The fourth is that as the child participates and develops and interacts with others and her or his environment, she or he must enjoy protection from harm and injury because of her or his vulnerability. Viewed in this way, the implementation of Article 5 requires a holistic approach to the child's rights. With regard to Article 6 of the CRC which underlines survival and development, for example, the CRC Committee has underlined that 'the right to survival and development can only be implemented in a holistic manner, through the enforcement of

---

[161] *Ibid.*, para. 8.
[162] G. Kamchedzera, *Access to Property, the Social Trust, and the Rights of the Child* (Cambridge; PhD Dissertation, unpublished, 1996).

all the provisions of the Convention, including rights to health, adequate nutrition, social security, and adequate standard of living, a healthy and safe environment, education and play.'[163] Similarly, the child's right to receive appropriate direction and guidance relates to all the other child rights, as goals for the progressive well-being and dignified life of the child.

3.4 The Manner of Direction and Guidance

64. Article 5 of the CRC's reference to 'appropriate' direction and guidance for the child invokes standards about the manner of performing the duties correlative to the child's right to receive direction and guidance. From a child rights-based approach, this signifies that not only must the direction and guidance be cognisant of the child's evolving capacities, but that it must also comply with child rights and other human rights principles.

65. The importance of complying with human rights principles in the provision, protection, facilitation and respect of the parental guidance has been recognized by the CRC Committee. In its General Comment on Early Childhood,[164] the Committee has underlined the need to advance the child rights principles it had earlier identified to guide States in their implementation of and reporting on the CRC.[165] The first, according to the Committee's characterisation, is the right to life, survival, and development, albeit more related to child rights goals. The second, non-discrimination, is indisputably a principle, as it applies to all the Articles and gives direction on issues of processes, systems, attitudes and approaches. The third is the principle that the best interests of the child must be a primary consideration in all decisions and actions that may affect the child. The fourth has long been presented as the 'respect for the views of the child.' However, to apply to all children and all the CRC's Articles, the principle may have to be restated to signify 'participation according to the child's evolving capacities.' Such a principle is most strongly embedded in Article 5 amongst the CRC's Articles.[166] Article 5 therefore provides a better basis of the principle than the traditionally presented Article 12 of the CRC. Indeed Article 12 relates more specifically to the formation and expression of views by the child.

---

[163] CRC Committee, *General Comment No. 7. Implementing Child Rights in Early Childhood, o.c.,* para. 10.

[164] *Ibid.*

[165] CRC Committee, *General Guidelines Regarding the Form and Content of Initial Reports to be Submitted by States Parties under Article 44, paragraph 1(a), of the Convention, o.c.*

[166] G. Lansdown, *o.c.*, p. 18.

66. Article 5 of the CRC is clear that appropriate direction and guidance must be consistent with the child's evolving capacities. This has two significations. The first is that the child, irrespective of age and situation, must be recognized as an active participator in her or his own development, a point noted by previous commentaries[167] and the CRC Committee.[168] This aspect of the CRC's Article 5 is potentially revolutionary, especially with regard to the rights of the young child. The CRC Committee explains the reason in the following terms:

> Respect for the young child's agency—as a participant in family, community and society, is frequently overlooked, or rejected as inappropriate on the grounds of age and maturity. In many countries and regions, traditional beliefs have emphasized young children's need for training and socialization. They have been regarded as undeveloped, lacking even basic capacities of understanding, communicating and making choices. They have been powerless within their families, and often voiceless and invisible within society.... As holders of rights, even the youngest children are entitled to express their views, which should be 'given due weight in accordance with the age and maturity of the child' (art.12.1).[169]

67. The CRC's image of the child as a participator in her or his well-being is increasingly substantiated by scientific evidence. A growing 'body of theory and research confirms that young children are best understood as social actors whose survival, well-being and development are dependent on and built around close relationships.'[170] Lansdown, joining other theorists and researchers,[171] for example, poignantly posits that like adults, 'children build competencies through direct experience.'[172]

68. The second signification of the principle of participation according to the child's evolving capacities is that parental guidance must both match and stimulate the child's capacities. Participation is essential for greater competence, which in turn requires increased participation. The child's

---

[167] S. Detrick, o.c., P. Alston, l.c., pp. 1–15; R. Hodgkin and P. Newell, o.c., pp. 85–94.

[168] CRC Committee, *General Comment No. 7. Implementing Child Rights in Early Childhood*, o.c.

[169] *Ibid.*, para. 14.

[170] *Ibid.*

[171] L.S. Vygotsky., *Mind in Society: The Development of Higher Psychological Processes* (London, Harvard University Press, 1978); L. Chawla and H. Heft, 'Children's Competence and the Ecology of Communities', *Journal of Environmental Psychology* 22, 2002, pp. 201–216; A.B. Smith., 'Interpreting and supporting participation rights: Contributions from socio-cultural theory', *International Journal of Children's Rights* 10, 2002, pp. 73–88; G. Lansdown, *Promoting Children's Participation in Democratic Decision-Making* (Florence, UNICEF Innocenti Research Centre, 2001); J. Miller, *Never too young: How Young children can Take Responsibility and Make Decisions* (London, National Early Years Network/Save the Children, 1997).

[172] G. Lansdown, o.c., section 3, p. 7.

progressive well-being or dignified life is adversely affected if this point is not recognized in the provision of appropriate direction and guidance. However, there is no case to stress that the need to allow participation to match and stimulate the child's evolving capacities is a licence for unlimited agency. Lansdown is correct to note that the principle or notion of the child's evolving capacities 'provides the framework for ensuring appropriate respect for children's agency without exposing them prematurely to the full responsibilities normally associated with adulthood.'[173] To attain such a balance, other child rights principles, particularly that the child's best interests must be a primary consideration in all decisions and actions, are instructive. The provisions of appropriate direction and guidance in this regard have to be characterized by a proper balance of the child's short and long term best interests. The perspective is that of the child's progressive dignified life, with the parents and carers approaching their roles as matters of duty. In this respect, Article 5 seriously challenges and limits the orthodox concept of parental autonomy.

69. This is a challenge that has so far been constitutionally welcomed by very few countries. Few jurisdictions have transcended the recognition of parental rights and duties to uniquely embrace the notion of the child's evolving capacities. In this regard, the constitutions of Finland, Poland, and Slovenia are illustrious. Finland's Constitution requires that children should 'be treated equally and as individuals and they shall be allowed to influence matters pertaining to themselves to a degree corresponding to their level of development.'[174] Poland's Constitution underlines that the upbringing of children must 'respect the degree of maturity of a child as well as his [her] freedom of conscience and belief and also his convictions.'[175] Slovenia's Constitution stipulates that parental guidance related to 'religious and moral upbringing' should be 'appropriate' to age and maturity.[176]

70. The framework for 'appropriate' provision of direction and guidance provided by Article 5 of the CRC is clear when viewed from the perspective of other child rights principles. The principle of the child's best interests becomes instructive and crucial, as it requires competence, prudence, and

---

[173] *Ibid.*, section 3, p. 3.

[174] Article 6(3) of the Constitution of Finland (1999), accessible through http://confinder.richmond.edu/.

[175] Article 48(1) of the Constitution of Poland (1997), accessible through http://confinder.richmond.edu/.

[176] Article 41 of the Constitution of Slovenia (1991), accessible through http://confinder.richmond.edu/.

fair-mindedness for the benefit of the child rather than the parent or care giver.

71. Further, instead of parental autonomy, the revolution demanded by the Article requires compliance with the principle of interdependence. This entails that the appropriate direction and guidance must recognize that all the child's rights are synergistic and the need for solidarity or interdependence in the performance of duties and the demanding of rights enjoyment. In a great sense, this means that the Article requires a relationship of interdependence between the parent or carer on the one side, and the child on the other.

72. Rather than blanket respect for parental autonomy, the principle of non-discrimination requires that the parent or carer must be fair to all children under her or his nurture. Attributes singled out by the CRC's Article 2, such as sex, must not be factors that result in favouritism in the provision of parental guidance. Evidence from countries such as Tanzania indicates that there is much discrimination in the family.[177] The human rights principle of equality entails that the State may, in certain cases, need to take priority actions for those parents and carers who are less able to provide appropriate direction and guidance.

73. The principle in the CRC that States must take appropriate steps or measures to the maximum extent for the implementation of the rights in the Convention is instructive. Appropriate measures and resources are respectively adopted and applied to advance the child's exercise of her or his rights by duty bearers at other societal levels, including at the household level. The provision and facilitation of parental guidance, furthermore, must promote accountability of duty bearers.

74. At the same time, the child's exercise of her or his rights must be responsible, in line with Article 29 of the Universal Declaration of Human Rights. In other words, the provision and facilitation of parental guidance must not result in the abuse, neglect and violation of the rights of others in society. The CRC has a few provisions that give examples of the limits in the enjoyment of certain rights.[178] However, Article 5 contains a general tenet placing trust in parents and carers that the child will be appropriately guided and directed.

---

[177] B. Rwezaura, *l.c.*
[178] *E.g.*, Articles 13, 14 and 15 of the CRC.

CHAPTER FOUR

CONCLUSION

75. The potential of Article 5 of the CRC to facilitate progressive dignified life for children has long been understated. This has largely been because of the obsession with families and parenthood. First, the child's right to appropriate direction and guidance has hitherto been unrecognized in previous commentaries on the CRC. Second, Article 5 is unique in international law, as it couples the importance of direction and guidance with the need to be responsive to the child's evolving capacities. Third, the notion of the child's evolving capacities has only recently started to gain recognition as a principle applicable to all other rights in the CRC. Participation according to the child's evolving capacities, however, is yet to replace the 'views of the child' as a child rights principle applicable to all the rights in the CRC and all children. Fourth, Article 5 well-captures the three factors that determine dignified life: what every person must enjoy, how every person should be treated, and what certain persons and bodies should do.

76. Article 5 is addressed to States, but the synergy of correlative duties whose performance is essential for the realisation of the child's rights encompasses all societal levels. Similarly, lower level duty bearers are rights holders against upper level duty bearers at all societal levels. It is the discharge of obligations at all societal levels and the demanding of rights enjoyment that is essential for the realisation of the child rights to appropriate direction and guidance. This entails sufficient capacities on part of both duty bearers and rights holders.

77. The Article's reference to 'appropriate' direction and guidance indicates the manner in which the direction and guidance by parents and key carers must be provided. The direction and guidance must match the child's capacities and contribute to the child's development. Further, the provision of the direction and guidance must advance and comply with child and other human rights principles. In addition, the direction and guidance must be responsive to the child as rights holder and key participator in her or his own survival, development, participation and protection. The Article's demand for 'appropriate' direction and guidance, the signification of correlative duties and duty bearers and rights holders at all societal levels, and

the stress of the child's evolving capacities are potentially transformative. If given effect, the Article will transform purposive relationships between the child, her or his key carers, the State, extended families, and communities to realize progressive dignified life. And in such a transformation, capacity development for the performance of duties and demanding of rights will be crucial.

SELECT BIBLIOGRAPHY

Archard, D., *Children's Rights and Adulthood* (London, Routledge, 2004).

Alston, P. and Tobin, J., *Laying the Foundations for Children's Rights* (Florence, UNICEF, 2005).

——, 'The Legal Framework of the Convention on the Rights of the Child', *91/2 United Nations Bulletin of Human Rights: The Rights of the Child* (1992), pp. 1–15.

Detrick, S. (ed.), *The United Nations Convention on the Rights of the Child: A Guide to the 'Travaux Préparatoires'* (London, Martinus Nijhoff Publishers, 1992), pp. 157–162.

——, *A Commentary on the United Nations Convention on the Rights of the Child* (The Hague, Martinus Nijhoff Publishers, 1999).

Eekelaar, J., Children Between Cultures', *International Journal of Law and the Family* 18, 2004, pp. 178–194.

Freeman, M. and Veerman, P. (eds.), *The Ideologies of Children's Rights* (London, Martinus Nijhoff Publishers, 1992).

Freeman, M., 'Taking Children's Rights More Seriously', *International Journal of Law and the Family* 6, 1992, pp. 52–71.

——, *The Moral Status of Children: Essays on the Rights of the Child* (London, Martinus Nijhoff, 1997).

——, 'Human Rights, Children's Rights and Judgement—Some Thoughts on Reconciling Universality and Pluralism', *The International Journal of Children's Rights* 10, 2002, pp. 345–354.

Giddens, A., *Runaway World* (London, Profile Books, 1999).

Hodgkin, R. and Newell, P., *Implementation Handbook for the Convention on the Rights of the Child* (New York, UNICEF, 2002), pp. 85–94.

Lansdown, G., *The Evolving Capacities of the Child*, (Florence, Save the Children and UNICEF, 2005).

Pinheiro, P.S., Independent Expert for the United Nations, Secretary-General's Study on Violence against Children, *World Report on Violence against Children* (Geneva, OHCHR, UNICEF, WHO, 2006).

Prout, A., *The Future of Childhood: Towards the Interdisciplinary Study of Children* (London/New York, Routledge Falmer, 2005).

Van Bueren, G., *The International Law of Child Rights* (The Hague, Kluwer Law International, 1998), chapter 3.

Van Nijnatten, C., 'Authority Relations in Families and Child Welfare in The Netherlands and England: New Styles of Governance', *International Journal of Law, Policy, and the Family* 14, 2000, pp. 107–130.

Woodhead, M., 'Early Childhood Development: a Question of Rights', (2005) *International Journal of Early Childhood* 37, No. 3, 2005, pp. 79–98.